# PASSPORT TO HERE AND THERE

GRACE NICHOLS

# Passport to Here
# and There

with photographs by
COMPTON DAVIS

BLOODAXE BOOKS

Copyright © Grace Nichols 2020
Photographs © Compton Davis 2020

ISBN: 978 1 78037 532 8

First published 2020 by
Bloodaxe Books Ltd,
Eastburn,
South Park,
Hexham,
Northumberland NE46 1BS.

www.bloodaxebooks.com
For further information about Bloodaxe titles
please visit our website or write to
the above address for a catalogue.

Supported using public funding by
ARTS COUNCIL
ENGLAND

Cover design: Neil Astley & Pamela Robertson-Pearce.

Printed in Great Britain by Bell & Bain Limited, Glasgow, Scotland, on
acid-free paper sourced from mills with FSC chain of custody certification.

*For my sisters and brother,*
*Avril, Valerie and Dennis*

# ACKNOWLEDGEMENTS

Acknowledgements are due to the editors of the following publications where a few of these poems or versions of them first appeared: 'Sweet Fifteen', *Jubilee Lines*, ed. Carol Ann Duffy (Faber & Faber, 2012); 'At Stockwell Station', *1914: Poetry Remembers*, ed. Carol Ann Duffy (Faber & Faber, 2014); 'The Shilling and the Princess', *Ploughshares* (USA) Spring 2015 translantic poetry issue, ed. Neil Astley; 'Battle', *Peace Poetry* to mark the centenary of Wilfred Owen published by the Royal Society of Literature (2018); 'O Tea', published in the 100th issue of *Wasafiri* (2019).

Special thanks to Victor Davson, Guyanese artist, whose painting, *White Christmas* is on the cover of this book, and to Compton Davis for his photographs of Georgetown. I would also like to thank Colin Grant who first drew to my attention the story of Howard Grey's photographs that emerged from the darkness, nearly 60 years after they were taken.

# CONTENTS

# Preface

One of the things we do as poets, is to try to preserve experiences, people, places important to us, in an effort to save them from time's erasure. In *Passport to Here and There*, I've been more conscious of this than in some of my other books and felt that a short introduction to my own background could make for some useful clarity.

Guyana (formerly British Guiana) gained its independence from Britain in 1966 after some 160 years of colonial rule. The only English-speaking country on the South American mainland, we're much closer, in terms of culture to the rest of the English-speaking cricket-playing Caribbean islands of Jamaica, Barbados, Trinidad etc and share with them an Atlantic coastline. But the history and myths of South America are still very much part of our imagination and consciousness, as is the influence of our own indigenous population, the Amerindians, who live in the forested areas of the country.

Before the British, Guyana was also colonised by the French and Dutch for varying periods. It was the Dutch 18th-century colonisers who built the much loved seawall to keep out the mighty Atlantic ocean along the coast. Georgetown and much of the coast are below sea level (as much as eight feet in parts) and the threat of the Atlantic, that sometimes come over at hightide in little brown splashes, is a real one, especially in view of global warming.

The Dutch also laid out the city with straight streets running beside flowing canals (somewhat like Amsterdam). These, together with tree-lined avenues, earned Georgetown the name, *Garden City of the Caribbean*. Georgetown itself lies within the county of Demerara, a name pregnant for most Guyanese since it not only evokes one of our main rivers, the Demerara, but also the brown sugar from the abundant canefields in that region.

Just under two years ago I made a return trip to Georgetown. It was my first time landing at Ogle, the smaller airport close to the city instead of the main airport in its foresty setting of Timehri, some 25 miles from the capital. As the plane sailed over the Atlantic and the lit-up capital, I was overwhelmed by it all. It was like seeing the city of my girlhood for the very first time.

As the two weeks went by I rediscovered Georgetown in many small ways – in the super-abundance of vegetables and familiar fruits at the market squares, the museum which we visited as children, walking on the seawall, re-meeting cousins and of course just catching up with my sisters and brother as we recalled childhood memories with laughter and sometimes tears. Those two weeks inspired what I've decided to call, 'Snapshot Sonnets', a coinage like the mingling of my English and Creole tongues, a playing with that most compulsive of forms, turning it towards a more anecdotal focus of memorable moments.

I wouldn't want to give the impression of Georgetown and Guyana being some kind of tropical idyll, as life for many Guyanese is a daily struggle and people still migrate when given the opportunity. Yet in recent years, a converse migration has been happening, since people from Venezuela, Brazil, Haiti, China, have all been settling in Guyana. And now that vast oil reserves have been found offshore (production has already started) who knows in what ways the country will change?

Growing up in Guyana (an Amerindian word that means, *Land of Many Waters*), my childhood seems to span two distinct periods. My early years were spent in the small coastal village of Stanleyville, but we called it Highdam, an ironic name since it was very flat.

I don't know whether it's wishful thinking on my part, but I believe I owe the fact I write at all to that village where I spent my 'small-girl days', stealing down to the shore with my sisters and brother, just before dawn, to catch crabs; catching fish in old baskets in our own backyard whenever it rained heavily. It was a magical amphibious kind of landscape, prone to flooding which was managed by man-made canals and dams and kokers, but the hot equatorial sun soon made it dry again once the kokers (a Dutch word for a kind of sluice) had drained away the water.

To this day I have this image of myself standing in brown water lit by the sun watching the shapes of fish go by below the surface. It is an enduring picture of myself caught in an innocent kind of cosmic bliss. For me the fish is like a living poem, a symbol of mystery that goes beyond itself and I subscribe to the English poet, Ted Hughes' view that as a poet you have to be able to fish your ideas from the sea of your unconscious.

My own love affair with language began with English nursery rhymes and fairy tales told by my mother, from Hansel and Gretel to Ali Baba and the forty thieves as well as our own frightening folk tales and jumbie (ghost) stories and nonsensical schoolyard rhymes.

Having moved to Georgetown at the age of eight, I joined the Public Free Library and was the proverbial bookworm. Enid Blyton, Richmal Crompton's William books (I adored William and his many escapades), Nancy Drew and Hardy Boys mysteries, were all grist for my young devouring imagination. The librarians tried in vain to get us to read more literary books but we simply went for what we liked.

I also liked dipping into my father's books of poetry. My father was a headmaster and our home was never short of books including those old Royal Readers he used at school with poems about soldiers dying on battlefields far from home, not to mention that boy *who stood on the burning deck whence all but he had fled*, experiences far removed from my world.

Nevertheless I remember being moved, not only by the emotions but by the images and music of the words. Later on in schools we had to study, as any student in England would have done, the works of Shakespeare, Keats, Wordsworth, Jane Austen, among others. It was only after coming to England that I came face to face with Wordsworth's iconic *Daffodil*, my favourite English flower by far.

*Passport to Here and There* attempts to give voice to the two cultures in terms of experience and textures that have helped to shape me as a person and as a poet, namely Guyana (within its Caribbean/South American context) and England and the historical bridges between them.

11

I've always been inspired by the actual physical landscape and now that I've been living in England for much longer than I've lived in Guyana, my sense of identity, my new-world-self has grown much more fluid. My Guyana-eye and Caribbean sensibility still filters my work but the Sussex landscape, the white chalk cliffs, the rolling downs which I enjoy walking on, the pagan mystery of the ancient hills, are all part of me now.

GRACE NICHOLS

# RITES OF PASSAGE

## If I Were to Meet

If I were to meet the ghost
of my childhood running
with slipping shoulder-straps
and half-plaited hair
beside a brown expanse
of memorising water
and the mellow faces of wooden houses
half-hidden by a weave
of coconut, mango, guenip trees.

I would say this was her childscape
this was where she was shaped
like first words formed on slate –

A raw and lyrical landscape
that witnessed her carelessness
of death, her fall from tree,
her near muddy-pool drowning
and how nothing seemed
to separate her from anything –
Not from the equatorial sun or sailing moon
or shooting stars of black tadpoles –

If I were to meet the ghost
of my childhood –
I would kneel beside her for a while –
this slip of a brown girl gazing at fish shapes
under brown sunlit water –
patwa, sunfish, butterfish –
mesmerised by their movement
and the silent scales of their music.

Then I'd straighten up
leaving her in her elementary world,
her bright aloneness. Oblivious of me.

# Litany

A litany that
still haunts the tongue –
a landscape
I cut my teeth on –
my muddy muse
in Atlantic gown

A pastureland
caught between flood
and the hard jigsaw
puzzle of drought
wide-eyed with waterview
and cosmic concern –

*Highdam/ Lowdam*
*Backdam/ Crabdam*

A piece of coast
an epoch, a brooch,
a gem of a jewel
I can still take out
to touch or dust
then for my own sake
put firmly away.

## Picture My Father

Picture my father, a seriously stylish
conducting headmaster,
waving his cane like a wand
pulling the length of the whole Methodist
Church School into singing –

*D'ye ken John Peel with his coat so grey*
*D'ye ken John Peel at the break of day*

Our Demerara voices rising and falling,
growing more and more golden
like a canefield's metamorphosis
from shoots into sugar,
the crystal memory shared with a river –

Our Demerara voices moving
to the magic of my father's wand,
flowing even more sweetly onto
that English maid deceived by some cad
in a valley below –

*O don't you leave me*
*O don't deceive me*

And me, stealing glances through the window
at our own rainwashed, sunbaked landscape.
And at my father, working
under all the accoutrements of empire.
Forty faithful years of being a teacher –

Handing out discipline, harmony, structure –
His gifts, unknown to me then.

# Greensleeves

And in the jalousied school-house next door
up to her elbows in prefeminist chores –
my mother – piano hands
sunk in the belly of a fish
scales rank and translucent
freckling the cinnamon of her skin.

Or rubbing clothes across the ribbed
bridge of a scrubbing board –
the sudden O of her lost soap
the indigo of her rinsing water –
the wind-scented pleasure of harvesting
them at the clothesline later.

Now witness her, head bent
over black and white keys
surprising the ear of the creole breeze
with that Tudor melody, *Greensleeves*.

# The Shilling and the Princess

Even now, I still remember
the pleading bribery
in my mother's eyes as she held out
the piece of silver in her palm –

A way figured out of the stress
of taking me down to Georgetown
to see the England-princess
in my new unfinished dress.

*'Which you prefer? To see the princess*
*or a Whole Shilling for yourself?'*
At six years old I took the silver
and betrayed the reality of it all –

The heaving crowds behind the barricades,
the cantering white horses, school children
waving little replicas of the British flag
(some fainting in the heat I later heard)

After she left I headed over to the cakeshop,
then watched the moon come up
like a fairy godmother
from behind the darkening trees.

Moon casting her mantling spell of silver –
making me most decidedly her goddaughter.

# Joy-riders

Evening, and the six o'clock beetles
come riding in on the wings
of the six o'clock wind

to do their nightly circuit
round and round the imaginary city
of our glowing country gas lamp –

until giddy from the excitement of it all
they begin to fall shiny and hard on their backs
like so many overturned black taxi cabs.

The following morning we'd sweep away
the wreckage, noting the little wheels
of their legs drawn up, burnt to a crisp.

Who knows where they came from –
these joy-riding ephemerals or why
like kamikaze pilots they choose a glittering death.

# Ole Higue

Should I tell you about our Ole Higue –
bane of the night rising
out of her wrinkled skin –
A fiery phoenix conjured
by us to ride the wind?

Well, hope yuh make
chalk-cross
outside your home

Hope yuh leave pile-of-rice
for she to count in case
she still slip – *floops* under the door.

Hope you dress yuh baby up
in blue nightie
scented with asofetida –

If daylight find she still counting
beat she with pointer-broom
yes kill the old blood-sucker.

But know that she already pass
her magic down in rich ochre soup
know that calabash is pledged
to silence by her blood in its gourd.

And that the rains will never
wash her footprints away –
In some moonlit storytelling backyard
our local vampire is reborn again.

# Masquerade

A straight-laced *Long-Lady*
swinging along sedately.
A twerking big-bamsey
*Bam-Bam Sally*
shaking more than what
she mother gave she.

But it's *Stilt-man*
our Atlantic faces
always return to –
held by his staggering
moves and form –
*Stilt-man* out to rival
the blue height of sky

In Boxing Day eruption
of dance and chanting colours
hypnosis of flute and drum –
footworks of small-boys
weaving the steps
of an ancient ritual –

And once again I am
spilling the hot coins
of my mother's silver
to the ground –
to appease the advancing
of that frightening
two-legged man-cow.

# Against the Tradewinds

Sitting sideways on the crossbar
of my father's *Raleigh* bicycle –
he pedaling, panting, pushing sixty
against the Tradewinds –
Me, in sulky pubescent silence –
a crossed-legged eleven-year old
offended by the implications
of his wind-snatched words:
*You're getting heavy girl*

# Confirmation

Suddenly, kneeling at the polished
wooden altar, palms cupped to receive
the body and blood of Christ – I felt it –
the imperceptible presence of something
like the fleeting shadow of a passover.

After the congratulatory hugs and kisses
welcoming us into the warm and sober
Methodist fold – I head off as if by instinct
to the sanctuary of the Ladies' Room
to confirm the arrival of my first moon

(thankfully hidden) behind the lining
of my white first-communion dress –
the tiny blooming stigmata
marking my own womanly ascent.

# A Chant for Mater

(Our next door neighbour whose kindness to
my mother after she suffered a stroke, remains
a beacon in my childhood memories)


Grace of goodness
in your silvery braids
milk of kindness –
in your rolling brown veins –
the bringer of fish stews

the star of the bark –
the grail of your footsteps –
a prayer in the dark.
Eternal madonna
mother to my mother –

May this praise reach you
on mountain or river
in valley or hillside
wherever you are –
Mater Mater.

## Sweet Fifteen

If the leaves of my memory serve me –
That was the year my hair went beehive
the year of the kiss, touching smugly
in the mirror my bee-stung lips.

If the branches of my memory stir me –
That was the year I fell in love with Otis,
each soulful syncopated syllable: *fa fa*
*fa fa fa fa fa fa* reverberating me to bliss.

For certain it was the year History rooted me –
Mr Owen, our history teacher – clad only in an armour
of trousers and rolled-up white sleeves, rescuing History
single-handedly from dates and dusty treaties.

Mr Owen giving the kiss-of-life to the leaden text –
Resurrecting from the pages the long gone dead –
Interweaving the Treaty of Tordesillas
with jokes about he and his dear Mrs Owen

Who always took such an age getting dressed,
that when she finally descends, all set,
he ascends to shave his grown-back beard again.
Then it was back to battles, islands claimed, renamed.

*Thank you, Mr Owen for the perks of your words*
*Thank you, Otis Redding for rocking my world*
*Thank you bee for my hive and my bee-stung lips*
*Thank you mirror for the buzz of that kiss.*

## Spirit-rising

All dressed-up with nowhere to go –
just propping-sorrow
on a holiday-Monday
at your Princess Street window.

Suddenly into this –
nothing-much-happening of a scene –
comes the unmistakable pulse
of a steelband beat and pretty soon
you can hear the tune

*Las' carnival ah had*
*a wonderful time*
*Archie bruk dem up*
*Archie bruk dem up*

Pretty soon you can see the prow
of the steelband-lorry
pulling behind a dancing crowd –
people jumping without a care
people ribbing up their waist
(commonplace people, as your
headmaster-father would say)

But the rhythm deep
and the music sweet
and the spirit already
taking possession of your feet.

And just so you breaking away –
down the passageway
oblivious of your father's command:

*'Come back here girl, I say, come back.'*
But all you can hear is the iron ringing
all you feel is the steel-God pulling.

And somehow you make a space
within a wave and you're quickly embraced –
warm chain of arms around
your neck and waist,
fastening you to the rhythm
to the hot muse of your people's spirit
in the heaving ship of music

*Las' carnival ah had*
*ah wonderful time*
*Archie bruk dem up*
*Archie bruk dem up*

How you dance entranced
mashing history up and down
in *The Garden-city-of-the-Caribbean* –
from Princess Street to Vlissengen Road
(still haunted with Dutch echoes)
from Vlissengen round Alberttown,
that district marked by an English crown

Then up past the Lamaha canal,
with Archie still ruling all –
only catching yourself up on the sea-wall
when an Atlantic wind bring
you back to the salt of your senses

*Yes, I took a chance*
*an' went to a dance,*
*Archie bruk dem up*
*Archie bruk dem up*

Now miles and years away
from that sacred hedonistic day
you smile at your fifteen-year-old self –
*that little mad woman*
as your father called her –
*still dancing in the dark.*

# Georgetown Romance

Set us loose in dis city
of wood and *tings hard bad*

Put a heap-of-crisscross streets
between us –
put traffic-light, road-block,
put seawall and canal.

Put iron railing
put hibiscus-paling
put clothesline
put coastline –

Because we so high on each other
Because we eyes can't wait
to make four together –
Dis not unfeeling city
will pull out all the stops
to bring us into each other's harbour.

# IN THE SHADE OF
# A LONDON PLANE TREE

# Viewing the Thames

Once they said you froze over, River,
and many walked on water transfigured
but I prefer you up and running Thames
with the flickering flames of your tales –
all London heaped up, a pop-up picture book –
spires, towers, bridges – a fine elation
for as yet I could see no dungeon
or abandoned blankets marking
the huddles of the homeless –
no aura of ghostly heads on spikes
that once festooned this London bridge
or trafficking vision of a phantom ship.
Just you, buoyant and open like the fluent
scrolls of Shakespeare's dog-eared manuscript.

# In the Shade of a London Plane Tree

The kind-house provided for my face
by your spirit's shade on this summer-hot day
wondering about your maple-like
leaves and the rings of your age
your spiked fruit-balls
that display themselves like pom-poms
stirred by an inaudible sway of music –
a merging of Oriental plane
and American sycamore – your hybrid
heart at home in any condition –
winter damp or heat-waving pollution –
a hardy Londoner if ever there was one.
Trees, how they intercede for us
in their green and breathing tolerance.

## O Tea

Like the heart that hungers for the perfect poem,
the palate hungers for the perfect cup of tea,
not unlike poetry, since the outcome will be
how it wants to be, a marriage of balance and taste
(a little more hot water, a bit more milk)
an alchemist, running on pure instinct –
O Tea that speaks of a leisurely
conviviality and a giving back to yourself
Tea that reaches the parts other brews can't
Tea that won't give you the quick
pick-me-uppedness of coffee
but will subtly change the chemistry of the blood.
Tea that will infuse you like an orchestra
infuses a great opera, which is of course yourself.

# Remember, Remember, the Fifth of November

*(Lewes Bonfire Night)*


Morning and the boarding up
of shop fronts begin –
in case of shoving crowds,
in case Prometheus's children
out to commemorate his hotly
stolen gift get out of hand.

Midday and kerosene invades the air
as ordinary townsfolk bloom
into Victorian and Tudor ladies,
fine-feathered Indians, Vikings, Zulus,
stripe-jerseyed busy bees
of bonfire girls and boys.

Nightfall and we're filling out the heaving streets –
craning our burning cheeks to see
within the bangers, sparks and brass,
the procession of lit torches
wheelbarrows of flaming logs
uneasy, soon to be burnt effigies.

And now the whole town reverberates –
crackling booms and flames.
The cold air gasps
at bright spells cast –
fountains of diamonds,
showers of falling stars.

Am I the only one to glimpse
at an upstairs window,
the pale face of a woman
drawing her curtains on it all –
as if she were the mother of a martyr
or one called Guy Fawkes?

# Robin Redbreast

No longer perched on the snowy
Christmas cards of my snowless childhood
but standing like a small feathered-muse
at my frosty garden door – Robin in the flesh
my *New-world, Old-world* friend – come to
warm me with the flame of his breast. Bless.

# Nuptial on Brighton Beach

As Sea gusts in
in veils of smoky grey
the seagulls descend
over the flaking balustrades –

Noisy bridesmaids
making their way behind
her bridal train of lacy foam
the shuffling guests of rolling stones

With raucous speeches
with feathered cries –
how they applaud this
wild and windy union of Sea and Sky.

# The Hills in Our Memory

*(in memory of Mary Hume)*


Mindful of the chalk-pit's edge, we'd take
the children onto the downs in Lewes early days.
Time, like the wheat fields, was generous then –

For blackberry picking and leisurely looking –
Snapshots in the Gambia.
Flapjacks in your Southover kitchen.

But Time sneaked up behind us
tightening its reins – our idle strolls,
impromptu picnics, growing less and less –

Yet the patchwork quilt of friendship
remained like the open downs of Sussex.
Restitching itself in unexpected

High Street meetings, in quick news exchanged.
Sometimes we snatched time back
for a cuppa at the White Hart –

Where I listened to your voice's octave.
Your unmistakable face, Mary –
The hills in our memory.

## Lewes Night Out

Night on the town of now quiet streets
free from the wheezing traffic that day breeds.
All ensconced in home. In pub –
embraced in the arms of Pelham and Brewers,
the White Hart, Black Horse, Snowdrop, the Gardener's –

Where at one time or other,
we've upped our fun
and downed our sorrows
for friends who went out like stars, pitching
their absence across the sky of our lives.

Down at the Lamb, see how we dance
to Neeta's yearly birthday bash –
old hippies, goths, glams, Pam and de Femmes,
we who are no longer spring-stepping lambs
still brave the steep cobbles of Keere Street –
not wisdom's choice in party heels.

Night on the town where history sleeps
dreaming of castle and battles
and bonfire leaps. Snuggling deep
into its patchwork quilt of downs
on whose breathing slopes the pagan past danced.
Hear the voice of the Ouse rivering the dark calm.

# Tea with Demerara Sugar

I've given up trying to give you up,
Demerara (not that I've ever tried).
Friends admonish me gently as they sip
their own unsweetened brew (ironically)
tucking into cakes far beyond me and you.
I say I've paid too high a price to give you up
and that just a teaspoon of you is enough
to brighten the tone of my tastebuds.
I know your cost in tears, brown sugar,
the bloody sweat behind each crystal grain –
you whose shadow still haunts the sun,
our riddling *water stand-up water lay down* –
turning me inward to my Demerara days,
your canetalk whispers fermenting the night air.

# Blackberrying Black Woman

Everyone has a blackberry poem. Why not this?
On a back road leading up to the Sussex downs
where the blackberries belong to no one –

A black woman is gathering in avid compulsion –
full-stretch against the summer sun –
the sweetfull promise of blackberries.

Lost in the berriness of it, oblivious
of passing glances and blackberry-lore
(the devil landed from heaven on this bushy briar).
The black woman – innocent as a newcomer –

Goes on picking the melodious blackberries
heedless of the blood from the prickling vine
as if pressed on by those giddying goblins
offering their succulent goblets of wine.

## Ode to a Daffodil

From where I'm sitting,
I can see you, daffodil,
if I turn towards the kitchen window.

Sometimes
you're a yellow-headed swan
about to sail off the grassy bank

Sometimes
a small chandelier
fostering a golden air

But when the wind blows
that's when you become –
an ambassador of the sun –

The way you nod
and sway,
head listeningly bent –

A radiating presence
pulling on the periphery
of my vision –

Happy to meet and greet
your earth-bound guests.

# Battle

Commissioned by the Royal Society of Literature to mark the 100th anniversary of the death of the English poet, Wilfred Owen, and inspired by his ironic war poem 'Dulce Et Decorum Est' ('sweet and honourable it is die for one's country').

Now on the sea-bed of childbirth
she gripped the iron railings
silently calling on her mother
and all the gods to help her –

Wave after wave
of shining pain breaking upon her –
her body an exhausted ship working
its way past the long haul of the siren's music –

O why can't the blood-gifted child spring from a rib
or burst like Athena from a father's forehead?

In her delirious distress, as each contraction
flares her back and gasps her breath
she thinks she sees Death
in the killing fields beyond the water-lights.

In the end, anchoring deep
in the inner trenches of herself –
just wanting it over and done with –
she pushed death back into the cupboard
and pushed Life – into the world –

Now years on, a grieving mother, she reflects:
'Was it for this that I endured what I endured?
To see the life I reared fed to the jaws
of some unwanted war, another bloody Troy,
primed with promises of sweet rewards?
O generations of lost sons!
My eyes the only flowers for an unknown grave.'

# This Destiny

To those West Indian émigrés who arrived at Waterloo Station in 1962, and to the photographer, Howard Grey, who'd captured them but who sadly felt he had failed to do so for when he tried to develop them, not a single picture emerged, just darkness. Remarkably nearly 60 years later, using enhanced digital scanners, the photographs flowered into the vivid present. There they were, the last batch of the *Windrush* generation to beat the Commonwealth Migration Act which would limit the entry of people from the British colonies to the UK.

Not seen. But there –
like the stored magic in a seed
that would one day flower –
they remained for over fifty years

A metaphor for endurance
a refusal to be erased, so they stayed
in the sublayer of themselves
awaiting the technology of a new age.

Waited until those high-definition
scanners beamed them up
into the light of their own flesh.
At last we could read their migration story –

All the details of their hopeful
anxious faces, clutched papers, against
the cold grey grains of a Waterloo station –
The last batch of empire's *Windrush* children

To put on their roosting-skates for Britain.
Clearly they'd ignored the advice
in the little booklet to British subjects
not to come dressed in their Sunday best –

For there they were – captured in space and time
in their bespoke coming-to-the-Motherland clothes –
tailored suits and ties, well-fitted dresses
and jackets made by some loved one left behind.

Now, like a gift you never knew you had –
the genius within your perceived failure
is revealed like this destiny –
out of the chrysalis of history.

# BACK-HOMING

### (GEORGETOWN SNAPSHOT SONNETS)

# Landing

The Liat plane dipping towards the rim
of Atlantic and the beginning of Georgetown
sends the wings unfurling from my heart
towards the city of my girlhood haunts,
Georgetown, shimmering in my new-spun eyes
with more lights than stars of night –
a coastal New York minus the skyscrapers –
Homing in to my first-time landing at Ogle,
nothing can stop my Demerara-smile
waxing wide as that sweetening estuary –
Not even the immigration officer,
who flicking through my British passport,
grants me exactly the fourteen days of stay
I'd asked for, in the country of my birth.

# Reunion

And even if no one had come to meet me
as I stepped out into the equatorial night
(baggage-burdened yet unbelievably light)
I would have probably grabbed and planted
a kiss on somebody – one of those homely
faces craning towards me like dark
expectant sunflowers in the waiting crowd –
staring unabashed at the reunion
of each emerging self-exiled arrivant.
But I spot them almost immediately –
my sisters and brother, Avril, Dennis, Valerie,
all the welcoming back-home rooted ones,
grounding us, as if we were returning
astronauts, in their arms of gravity.

## Where Blue Sea Turns

Yet I missed the familiar smells coming down
to the city from the main airport at Timheri –
nestling somewhere between the coastal plain
and green beginning of the Amazon –
that pregnant foresty air of earth and rain
as you drive along the old East Bank,
the flowing symphony of the Demerara
glimpsed behind the houses and trees,
that pungency passing Diamond Estate
(I refuse to say stench) like a beloved's
intimacy mingling with sugar and rum –
telling you without a doubt that you're
no longer in the archipelago of islands
but here where blue sea turns welcoming-brown.

# Bourda

Marvel again at the market stalls
singing the earth's abundance
in the heaped-up homegrown freshness
of their own vernacular favoured names.

Not Aubergine but Balanjay
     Not Spinach but Calaloo
Not Green-beans but Bora
     Not Chilli but Bird-pepper
And not just any mango
     but the one crowned, Buxton Spice,

Still hiding its ambrosia in the roof
of my mouth, still flowering
like the bird-picked mornings
on the branches of my memory.

# Where My Childhood Left Him

Nothing then, but to seek refuge from
the chaos of Stabroek Market Square
and the melting gold of the Eldorado sun
and dive into the cool ambience
of the Georgetown Museum – surfacing
among the glass cabinets of its stilled creation
drawn from the artistry of forest trees and rivers.
Like walking swimmers we re-acquaint with
Arapaima (world's biggest freshwater fish)
Great Harpy-eagle, the startling Hoatzin bird.
And standing exactly where my childhood left him –
old gold-seeking, diamond-dreaming, Pork-knocker –
saucepan and cutlass still hanging from his waist
still ready to chop brooding bush and stake his claim.

*Pork-knocker*, one of those rugged men who go into the forested interior of
Guyana prospecting for gold and diamonds. They took rations of salted pork
which they 'knocked back', slang for eating with relish. Hence, pork-knockers.

# El Hombre del Oro

*(The golden one)*

I swear, Sun has grown more bare-face
ever since we've managed to pull away
the fine fabric of his handkerchief –
the one with which he used to mop his brow
and shade in shadow his own magnificent glare.
Now like a true Amazonian warrior
Sun unleashes the flames of his keener arrows.
But don't imagine we've uncovered
all the rituals behind his horizon's clouds –
like the way he gold-dusts his skin each day
before entering that lake to bathe and pay
homage to the daemonic-goddess within,
*El Hombre del Oro*, our only Eldorado
who keeps us in the swim of his cosmic spin.

# From the Balcony of Eldorado

From the balcony of Eldorado
(the modest hotel where I'm staying)
I wonder about the hollow-eyed
yet dignified old house across the street,
its gap-toothed abandoned expression
among the well-kept colonial elders –
those stately white wooden houses intact
with Demerara windows, fretwork, jalousies.
If I strain my eyes I can almost see
the ghostly family of the wind moving
within that enduring shell-of-an-old-house.
Can almost hear its hallowed-prayer
for returning footsteps within the twin
seasons of rioting sun and rain.

# Price I Pay

Sorry for the big men walking up and down
the sweltering pavements trying to sell
mosquito-nets that nobody wants,
the white mesh rolled up like bridal
diaphragms in their arms. But I staying
in an air-conditioned hotel cushioned
against the advances of those serenading
whining and dining on blood musicians.
On my third morning at the Eldorado
however, I see I've acquired in the mirror,
the usual unasked-for-necklace of love-bites.
Despite my mosquito-repellant spray
(the love-price I must always pay)
for this bonding of skin – this back-homing.

# In the Fleeting Now

Still we venture out, two deranged aunties,
opening umbrellas against the searing glory
of a midday sun, me and my eldest sister –
always up for the lift of laughter –
despite her more-than-fair-share of sorrows.
In the avenue of flamboyant trees
I recount some risqué memory just to trigger
her clutched chest and shaking shoulders.
Soon we're two wilting flowers sitting
over glasses of coconut water –
Thankful for this day in which the only
breaking news is us, breaking the bread
of our deepest words as we revive
in the fleeting now of Time's eye.

## Like an Heiress

Like an heiress, drawn to the light of her
eye-catching jewels, Atlantic draws me
to the mirror of my oceanic small-days.
But the beach is deserted except for a lone
wave of rubbish against the old seawall –
used car tyres, plastic bottles, styrofoam cups –
rightly tossed back by an ocean's moodswings.
Undisturbed, not even by a seabird,
I stand under the sun's burning treasury
gazing out at the far-out gleam of Atlantic,
before heading back like a tourist
to the sanctuary of my hotel room
to dwell in the air-conditioned coolness
on the quickening years and fate of our planet.

# Eldorado

The young men liming about the street
corners worry the corners of my own eyes
seemingly caught in an old familiar dance.
Some will take migration chance,
some risk malaria in the hinterland,
where the dream of Eldorado still hangs –
a misty caul over the green secretive face
of forest. Eldorado, long-lost city of gold
that drew so many into its feverish folds
including Raleigh whose head eventually rolled
to the thunder of the executioner's axe
when he could not transform the breathing
alchemy of myth into caratted gold
or quench the fire of its timeless lure.

## Sorry

Sitting in a rocking minibus
beside a shirtless man in dreadlocks.
Each time the bus swings you pitch against him
offering a *sorry* at each encounter of skin.
At the third, he gets into a huff:
*'Wha yuh sarry fa?'* You'd forgotten
that too much politeness, too many *sorries*
(for which you secretly blame the English)
only get your people irritated.
Might as well beg pardon for breathing
keeping yuhself to yuhself,
afraid to big-up yuhself and spread.
There is much in life to be sorry about.
Pressing against a bicep isn't one of them.

## Against My Heart

Passing the city cemetery, Le Repentir,
I see that the dead, in lieu of homage,
have been busy planting all manner
of vegetation from their unkempt graves.
Hibiscus flowers to gladden the eye.
Irrepressible grass to cushion the feet.
The stately sentinels of palm trees
to guard their everlasting sleep.
Throughout my stay, in sun, in shade,
I make no attempt to trace the graves
of my long-lost loved ones – they who swim
within the pilgrimage of my blood.
They who can hear their epitaph
if they placed their heads against my heart.

# Georgetown

In the silent blooming of memory
I picture us both young – I clutching
my precious library books down
your flame-petalled avenues that once
deemed you *Garden City of the Caribbean* –
the red bells of your hibiscuses
ringing me through to adulthood.
What can you do now, Georgetown,
but accept the newly sprung up
concrete monstrosities beside
your mellow timbered-beauty,
your blocked arteries of canals and alleys?
What can I do but hold fast, Seawall-city,
to your below-sea-level courage?

# INTERESTING TIMES?

# Interesting Times?

May you live in interesting times.

TRADITIONAL CHINESE CURSE

Such interesting times we live in
we put on the TV and swear
it's some drama being played
till we detect that the maniac air is real.

Such interesting times, that the shroud
of silence over the *Why and Wherefore*
of a tower block's flammable cladding,
is more pregnant than the sound of sirens –

Such interesting times, such cunning times,
that we cannot find, not even
with an inward eye, the space that holds
the numbness of our collective grief –

What song of mourning can I sing, Grenfell?
What words of solace for wounds so deep?

# At Stockwell Tube

Remembering the young Brazilian who was mistaken for a
terrorist and shot at Stockwell Tube Station in London.


Death followed you to the underground.
Followed you, Jean Charles de Menezes,
even onto this train – but no trace
of your blood now. No flowering stain.
Just this palpable vision of an oblivious gun
pressed against your bewildered terror.

What if it's the wrong man? I remember
asking, Death, what if he's innocent?

But Death, heedless of my Cassandra words,
followed you to the underground,
followed you to a world gone all wrong –
A metal sky, a fabricated earth, no carnival.
Just unstoppable Death in the shape of the law
and a mother journeying to the root of her tears.

# In Praise of Surgeons

*(for Peter Larsen-Disney and for the NHS)*


Sometimes, lying in the quiet dark,
I trace again the careful cut you made
and think we should be kissing
the hands of surgeons everywhere –
you who work with knife and thread
and blood and understand
how our fragile flesh is strung.
Yes, sometimes, lying in the quiet dark,
I think of you, Peter Larsen-Disney,
and bless your hands and that fine
precise almost non-existent scar you left
just below the bikini line of my belly.
For you this song is sung.

# Kittitian Girl

*(for Zelma)*


Your departures stir a longing
for your comeback arrivals –
you who left your island home
to follow your heart's nursing vocation
on England's distant shore.

But you needed no lamp like Florence
Nightingale to see your way to heal.
No Crimea like Mary Seacole
as you scaled duty's rungs
with a smile to console the snow.

Kittitian girl, we marvel at the ease
with which you juggle
the love of your two homes –
bearing generous witness.
Loyal to both sides of Atlantic.

# Faith

*(An acrostic for Simon and Imtiaz)*

It wasn't Cupid, but rather
Madam Faith who came
To wrap you both in her
Invisible cape –
Awaiting with you a taxi's U-turn. Would it
Zoom back with a black bag intact?
She stayed calm. He was hopeful yet concerned.
Indeed as he spoke on his mobile phone
Mumbai shifted a little closer to home.
O would his generous tip save her live poetry?
Never did a lost bag share a sweeter story.

# Helen of the Gables

What are birthdays for if not to cast
a glow around her being in the world –
this Welsh-born girl still carrying a bit
of the Boudicca warrior-gene in her?

When a group of Muslim women looking
for somewhere to pray in hilly Lewes,
stop her for directions in their car,
how does our Helen respond?

Not by pointing towards some distant Troy
but by ushering them across the threshold
into the spontaneous Mecca of her own home –
the *Gables*, as it's known.

Now like a human face
the *Gables* meditates on a day
its roof knew minarets –
and a wind circled in like a pilgrimage –

And the hearth lit up of its own accord,
as we are, by the quick of Helen's heart.

## To Mark Your Passing
*(for Derek Walcott)*


To mark your passing into the arms
of everlasting sleep and to console ourselves
against the tyranny of Time and Death –
your books (the ones we've taken from the harbour
of our shelves) now lie about the house –
The treasured cargo of our inheritance.

On the dining table where I work,
the sea-washed *Omeros*,
on the sofa *The Arkansas Testament*
with its frigate-bird cover,
in the bedroom, your wind-ruffled *Selected*,
against the bathroom wall, what else but *White Egrets?*

Even as the whole house fills
with *The Joker of Seville* and regrets –
your shimmering Caribbean-infused lyrics
interwoven with MacDermot's sublime music –

*O River Manzanares*

We who never told you face up
of your worth to us in words
or wove any garland of flowers
to place around your forehead
yet audacious as we are, saw you,
though you belong to the world, as ours.

Contemplating you more like a distant sea-god
on the shores of our consciousness,
one who had painted our virginal world
in lyrical and heaped-up textures.

When last I saw you at Shakespeare's Globe,
that performance of *Omeros*,
I remember how in one last ditched effort,
I lent over your wheelchair
to whisper close to your ear
*You are our Caribbean Shakespeare.*

As always, I was too late.
Your grey-green eyes gave the faintest
of flickers but were already elsewhere –
beyond the hills. Over the fields of sugarcane.
In any case you were your own child prodigy
penning your verses to the metre of the sea.

So today, in memorial, in memory,
I giving thanks, Derek,
for the tight-rigged schooners of your lines
for the rivers of your stanzas
for the *Amen* of your calm St Lucian waters.

# A Sacrament of Words

*(for Guyanese poet, Martin Carter)*

Walking slowly in the wind
like your cartman of dayclean,
pushing one-one against
the stars and scars of a city
whose altars knew hands like yours.

Your words, Georgetown-man, priest-man,
marrying canna-lilies to canals,
city flames to ocean floods,
berating the shining
governments of the damned.

Drinking from an anguished chalice
yet placing the hopeful sacrament
of words – star, seed, flower
on our tongues. Sharing the wine
of your imperishable spirit.

Like Akhmatova wading her grief
through the snows of deepest Russia,
you did not leave, Martin,
but stayed to keep your ear to the ground.
Your heart to our city's pulse.

# Lost in Translation
*(por el espíritu de poesía en Medellín, Colombia)*


As if the earth had shifted axis again
I walk the streets of your city, Medellín,
a hammock of memories swinging in my head –
these streets where Escobar's ghost still dwell.

At the market-square, between the flowing
symphony of sun and rain, I sample
the bribery of coffee poured
from flasks into little plastic cups;

Pure Colombian gold I'm told.
In return I buy an indigenous looking
T-shirt, sliced mangoes,
shiny avocados of my childhood.

But the people's desire for poems,
the people who listened to our utterance
against the Andean elements –
thunder, lightning, rain –

And my own bouts of pan-pipe sickness
for a continent I'd lost
despite the richness of English –
Where did that come from?

I want to bridge this gap of tongues
between us, Medellín. I want to hear
my voice rolling like a river over
the Spanish syllables of your question;

*¿Estás contenta?*
*Sí, estoy muy, muy, contenta.*

# Apple and Mango

When last home, trying to recover
some of the bright light of small-girl days,
my sister threw me the sudden gift
of a Buxton Spice mango.

I remember how I peeled and sliced
that plump orb of sunshine,
adding a sprinkling of salt,
the way I liked it as a child.

I remember how she raised her eyes
when I said I'd leave back for *afters*, a slice –
*Girl, you can't finish one mango?*

How could I have admitted
that I had to save back space
for the fruits of my other back-home –

This rain and winter-driven Blighty
where summery strawberry
and apple and my daughters all grow.

# Rivers

*(for Frank Bowling, Guyanese-British artist)*

No wonder your paintings
carry the genes of rivers
born as you were
in a land of many waters

No wonder your veins
can't escape their openness –
whether the unscrolling Thames
or mighty-mapping Essequibo –
the silken memory goes deep
within your childhood bones

As you translate for us
their liquid language
in the ebb
      and flowing drama
of your own colour instinct –

In living breath
of violet   magenta
flamingo-pink   winter-green
burning sienna –
*And Who's afraid*
*of Red, Yellow and Blue?*

Not you, Bartica boy,
alchemist –
you who are yourself the gift
of colour's mystic form and mist.

# Dawn Wind

*(for Guyana-born artist, Victor Davson)*


Dipping your brush
with luminous wings
into river-memory –

You bring Dawn Wind to the mouth
of Eliot's brown god
giving form to a poet's line

Or is it the changing faces of Atlantic
its rustic sheen and shadow rippling
across your canvas like roofs of galvanise?

Colours that cannot leave you, Victor,
born as they are in the cauldron
of your Demerara eyes.

# Atlantic

Married as we were to your brown
untourist beaches, unconcerned
with the many shores you touched,
as children, we thought that you, Atlantic,
belonged to us, your below-sea-level offspring.

See us playing cricket,
turn-down bucket making wicket –
ball a spin-off of empire –
lost in the applauding waves for six.
At Easter, to mark the ascent of Christ,
see us raising a carnival of butterflying kites.

Yet we know that playfulness is not your nature
that ships sink in you like matchsticks
that small boys daring to dive from the jetty's edge,
sometimes never surface –
from your majestic, magnetic depths.

So from the seawall's Dutch-built safety,
we watched your changing moods
your glimmers and your gloom.

Atlantic – now sleeping in the distance
peaceful as a dog glossed by the morning sun.
Atlantic – now churning up an army of wild horses,
white manes threatening a biblical leaping
or brooding on the ships that bruised your memory –
the nameless bones on the sea-shelves of your history.

Still, at dusk, we love to sit in the evenings' calm
hearing the wash of your voice over rocks and sand –
watching the small emergence of a blue-back crab.
Me thinking that is you, Atlantic, who give birth
in the nascent dark, to the coming-on stars.